EMMANUEL JOSEPH

From Farm to Fork to Factory, The Role of Robotics and Society in Food Evolution

Contents

1

Chapter 1: The Dawn of Agriculture

In the nascent days of agriculture, humanity transitioned from a nomadic lifestyle to one rooted in cultivating crops and domesticating animals. This monumental shift set the stage for the development of societies and civilizations. Early farmers employed rudimentary tools and techniques to enhance productivity, though it was an era defined more by sheer effort than efficiency.

With agriculture came the first signs of community, as people settled near fertile lands. These burgeoning societies began to share knowledge, leading to incremental improvements in farming methods. Crop rotation, irrigation, and selective breeding marked the evolution of agricultural practices. Every innovation was a step toward ensuring food security and supporting larger populations.

Despite these advancements, farming remained labor-intensive and at the mercy of nature. Droughts, floods, and pests could devastate entire crops, posing significant risks to early agricultural societies. The constant battle against the elements and the struggle to sustain the community forged a deep connection between people and their land.

As societies grew, so did the complexity of agricultural practices. Specialized roles emerged within communities, leading to the development of early agricultural economies. These early steps laid the groundwork for future technological innovations, setting humanity on a path toward modern food production.

2

Chapter 2: The Industrial Revolution and Mechanized Agriculture

The Industrial Revolution of the 18th and 19th centuries was a transformative period that introduced mechanization to agriculture. The advent of steam power and machinery revolutionized farming, increasing efficiency and productivity. Innovations such as the seed drill, mechanical reaper, and threshing machine allowed farmers to cultivate and harvest larger areas with less labor.

The introduction of mechanized equipment transformed the agricultural landscape. Tractors replaced horses and oxen, enabling farmers to plow fields more quickly and plant crops with greater precision. This era marked a significant shift from manual labor to machine-driven agriculture, reducing the physical strain on farmers and increasing the scale of production.

The increased efficiency of mechanized agriculture led to surplus production, which in turn spurred the growth of the global food trade. Crops could be grown in one region and transported to another, connecting distant markets and diversifying diets. This period also saw the rise of agribusinesses, as farming became more commercialized and profit-driven.

While mechanization brought numerous benefits, it also introduced new challenges. Small-scale farmers struggled to compete with large, industrialized operations. The environmental impact of intensive farming practices began to surface, raising concerns about sustainability and the long-term health of the land. Despite these issues, the Industrial Revolution set the stage for further advancements in agricultural technology.

3

Chapter 3: The Green Revolution

The mid-20th century witnessed the Green Revolution, a period characterized by the widespread adoption of high-yield crop varieties, synthetic fertilizers, and advanced irrigation techniques. Spearheaded by scientists like Norman Borlaug, the Green Revolution aimed to address global food shortages and improve agricultural productivity, particularly in developing countries.

High-yield crop varieties, such as dwarf wheat and rice, were engineered to produce more grain per plant and resist diseases. These crops, combined with the use of chemical fertilizers and pesticides, significantly increased food production. The Green Revolution brought about dramatic improvements in crop yields, helping to alleviate hunger and malnutrition in many parts of the world.

Advanced irrigation techniques, such as drip irrigation and sprinkler systems, further enhanced agricultural productivity. These methods allowed for more efficient water use, reducing waste and ensuring that crops received the necessary moisture to thrive. The Green Revolution also promoted the use of mechanized equipment, further boosting efficiency and output.

However, the Green Revolution was not without its drawbacks. The heavy reliance on chemical inputs raised concerns about environmental degradation, soil depletion, and the loss of biodiversity. Small-scale farmers often struggled to afford the necessary inputs, leading to increased economic

disparity. Despite these challenges, the Green Revolution had a profound
impact on global food production and set the stage for future innovations.

4

Chapter 4: The Advent of Precision Agriculture

In recent decades, the agricultural sector has seen the rise of precision agriculture, a technology-driven approach that leverages data and advanced tools to optimize farming practices. Precision agriculture aims to increase efficiency, reduce waste, and enhance sustainability by providing farmers with real-time information about their crops and fields.

One of the key components of precision agriculture is the use of GPS technology. GPS-enabled equipment allows farmers to map their fields with pinpoint accuracy, enabling precise planting, fertilization, and harvesting. This level of precision helps to reduce input costs and minimize environmental impact by applying resources only where they are needed.

Remote sensing technologies, such as drones and satellite imagery, provide farmers with valuable insights into crop health and soil conditions. These tools can detect early signs of pest infestations, nutrient deficiencies, and water stress, allowing farmers to take timely action. By monitoring their fields from above, farmers can make informed decisions that improve crop yields and resource management.

Precision agriculture also incorporates data analytics and machine learning to analyze vast amounts of information. By processing data from various sources, these technologies can identify patterns and trends, providing farmers with actionable insights. This data-driven approach enables farmers to optimize their practices, increase productivity, and promote sustainable agriculture.

5

Chapter 5: Robotics in the Field

The integration of robotics into agriculture has ushered in a new era of efficiency and innovation. Agricultural robots, or "agrobots," are designed to perform a variety of tasks, from planting and harvesting to weeding and monitoring crop health. These machines are revolutionizing the way farmers manage their fields and produce food.

One of the most significant advancements in agricultural robotics is the development of autonomous tractors and harvesters. These machines can operate without human intervention, using GPS and sensor technology to navigate fields with precision. Autonomous equipment can work around the clock, increasing productivity and reducing labor costs.

Robotic systems are also being used to improve planting and crop care. Precision planters can sow seeds at optimal depths and spacing, ensuring uniform growth and maximizing yields. Robotic weeding machines use advanced imaging technology to identify and remove weeds, reducing the need for chemical herbicides and promoting sustainable farming practices.

In addition to fieldwork, robots are playing a crucial role in monitoring crop health. Drones equipped with multispectral cameras can survey large areas of farmland, capturing detailed images that reveal plant stress and disease. Ground-based robots can collect soil samples and analyze nutrient levels, providing farmers with real-time data to make informed decisions. The continued advancement of agricultural robotics promises to enhance efficiency, sustainability, and food security.

$$6$$

Chapter 6: The Rise of Vertical Farming

As urbanization and population growth continue to strain traditional agricultural systems, vertical farming has emerged as a viable solution for producing food in densely populated areas. Vertical farming involves growing crops in stacked layers, often within controlled environments such as greenhouses or indoor facilities. This innovative approach maximizes space and resources, allowing for year-round cultivation.

One of the key benefits of vertical farming is its ability to produce high yields in a small footprint. By utilizing vertical space, farmers can grow multiple layers of crops in a single location, significantly increasing productivity. This method is particularly valuable in urban areas where land is scarce and expensive.

Controlled environment agriculture (CEA) is a fundamental aspect of vertical farming. By carefully regulating factors such as temperature, humidity, light, and nutrient levels, vertical farms can create optimal growing conditions for crops. This precision control minimizes the risk of pests and diseases, reduces water usage, and eliminates the need for chemical pesticides and herbicides.

Vertical farming also promotes sustainability by reducing the distance food must travel from farm to table. Locally grown produce can be harvested at peak ripeness and delivered to consumers within hours, ensuring fresher and more nutritious food. As technology continues to advance, vertical farming holds the potential to revolutionize urban agriculture and contribute to global food security.

7

Chapter 7: The Impact of Genetic Engineering

Genetic engineering has had a profound impact on agriculture, enabling scientists to modify the genetic makeup of crops to enhance their traits and performance. This technology, often referred to as genetic modification or GM, has led to the development of crops that are more resistant to pests, diseases, and environmental stresses, as well as those with improved nutritional content.

One of the most notable examples of genetic engineering in agriculture is the development of Bt crops. These crops have been genetically modified to produce a protein derived from the bacterium Bacillus thuringiensis (Bt), which is toxic to certain insect pests. Bt crops, such as corn and cotton, have reduced the need for chemical insecticides, leading to more sustainable and environmentally friendly farming practices.

Genetic engineering has also played a crucial role in enhancing crop resilience. Scientists have developed drought-tolerant and salt-tolerant varieties that can thrive in challenging conditions. These crops are particularly valuable in regions prone to extreme weather events and soil degradation, helping to ensure food security in the face of climate change.

In addition to pest and stress resistance, genetic engineering has been used to improve the nutritional quality of crops. Biofortified crops, such as Golden

Rice, have been engineered to contain higher levels of essential nutrients like vitamin A and iron. These crops have the potential to address malnutrition and micronutrient deficiencies in vulnerable populations, contributing to better public health outcomes.

8

Chapter 8: The Role of Artificial Intelligence

Artificial intelligence (AI) is transforming agriculture by providing farmers with powerful tools to analyze data, optimize processes, and make informed decisions. AI-driven technologies are enhancing productivity, sustainability, and resilience in the agricultural sector, paving the way for a more efficient and connected food system.

One of the key applications of AI in agriculture is predictive analytics. By analyzing historical and real-time data, AI algorithms can forecast crop yields, pest outbreaks, and weather patterns. These insights enable farmers to take proactive measures, such as adjusting planting schedules, applying targeted treatments, and managing resources more effectively.

AI-powered automation is also making significant strides in the field. Autonomous drones and robots equipped with AI technology can perform tasks such as planting, fertilizing, and monitoring crops with high precision. These machines can operate 24/7, reducing the need for manual labor and increasing efficiency. Additionally, AI-driven systems can detect and respond to issues in real-time, preventing potential crop losses and improving overall farm management.

Another important aspect of AI in agriculture is decision support systems. These platforms use AI algorithms to analyze data from various sources and provide farmers with actionable recommendations. Whether it's determining the optimal time to harvest or identifying the best crop varieties for a particular region, AI-driven decision support systems help farmers make informed choices that maximize productivity and sustainability.

9

Chapter 9: The Emergence of Food Tech Startups

The food industry is experiencing a wave of innovation driven by a new generation of food tech startups. These companies are leveraging cutting-edge technologies to address various challenges in the food supply chain, from production and distribution to consumption and waste management. The emergence of food tech startups is reshaping the way we think about and interact with food.

One area where food tech startups are making a significant impact is alternative proteins. Companies like Beyond Meat and Impossible Foods are developing plant-based and lab-grown meat products that mimic the taste and texture of traditional meat. These innovations aim to reduce the environmental impact of livestock farming, improve animal welfare, and provide consumers with sustainable protein options.

Another focus of food tech startups is food waste reduction. Companies like Apeel Sciences and Too Good To Go are developing solutions to extend the shelf life of fresh produce and reduce food waste in households and businesses. By tackling food waste at various stages of the supply chain, these startups are contributing to a more sustainable and efficient food system.

Food tech startups are also exploring new ways to enhance food safety and traceability. Blockchain technology, for example, is being used to create transparent and tamper-proof records of food production and distribution. This technology helps to prevent food fraud, ensure product authenticity, and improve recall processes in the event of contamination. The rise of food tech startups is driving innovation and creating new opportunities in the food industry.

10

Chapter 10: The Intersection of Food and Society

The evolution of food production and technology has profound implications for society. Food is not just a basic necessity; it is deeply intertwined with culture, identity, and social structures. The changes brought about by advancements in agriculture and food technology are reshaping our relationship with food and influencing various aspects of society.

One of the key social implications of food evolution is the shift in dietary patterns. The availability of diverse and convenient food options has transformed eating habits, leading to the rise of fast food, processed foods, and ready-to-eat meals. While these options offer convenience, they also raise concerns about health and nutrition. The prevalence of diet-related diseases, such as obesity and diabetes, highlights the need for a balanced and informed approach to food consumption.

Food technology is also playing a role in addressing food insecurity and malnutrition. Innovations such as fortified foods, biofortified crops, and meal delivery services are helping to provide nutritious and affordable food to vulnerable populations. These efforts are contributing to the fight against hunger and promoting better health outcomes worldwide.

Moreover, the cultural significance of food is evolving as technology changes the way we produce and consume it. Traditional farming practices and local cuisines are being influenced by global trends and technological advancements. This dynamic interplay between tradition and innovation is shaping new food cultures and creating opportunities for cross-cultural exchange and collaboration.

11

Chapter 11: Sustainability and the Future of Food

As the global population continues to grow, ensuring the sustainability of our food systems is becoming increasingly critical. The future of food will depend on our ability to balance productivity with environmental stewardship, resource conservation, and social equity. Sustainable agriculture and food production are essential for meeting the needs of current and future generations.

One of the key pillars of sustainable agriculture is the adoption of regenerative farming practices. Regenerative agriculture focuses on restoring soil health, increasing biodiversity, and sequestering carbon in the soil. Practices such as cover cropping, no-till farming, and agroforestry help to build resilient ecosystems and reduce the environmental impact of farming.

Another important aspect of sustainability is reducing the carbon footprint of food production and distribution. Innovations such as renewable energy, precision agriculture, and vertical farming are helping to minimize greenhouse gas emissions and improve resource efficiency. By embracing sustainable technologies and practices, the food industry can contribute to climate change mitigation and environmental protection.

Consumer behavior also plays a crucial role in shaping the future of food. Increasing awareness about the environmental and social impact of food choices is driving demand for sustainable and ethically produced products. Consumers are seeking transparency, traceability, and accountability in the food supply chain, prompting businesses to adopt more sustainable practices and prioritize social responsibility.

12

Chapter 12: The Role of Robotics in the Food Industry

The integration of robotics in the food industry is revolutionizing the way we process, package, and deliver food. From automated production lines to robot-assisted kitchens, robotics is enhancing efficiency, consistency, and safety across various stages of the food supply chain. The role of robotics in the food industry is expanding, offering new possibilities for innovation and growth.

In food processing and manufacturing, robots are being used to perform tasks such as slicing, dicing, and packaging with high precision and speed. These machines can handle repetitive and labor-intensive processes, reducing the risk of human error and contamination. Automated production lines also enable manufacturers to scale up operations and meet the demands of a growing market.

Robotic technology is also making its way into commercial kitchens and restaurants. Robot chefs and automated cooking systems can prepare meals with consistent quality and taste, streamlining food preparation and reducing wait times. These innovations are particularly valuable in high-volume settings, where efficiency and speed are paramount.

In the realm of food delivery and logistics, robotics is transforming the way we get food from farm to fork. Autonomous delivery robots and drones can transport food orders directly to consumers' doorsteps, offering convenience and reducing delivery times. Additionally, robots equipped with AI and machine learning can optimize supply chain management, ensuring that food reaches its destination fresh and on time.

As robotics continues to advance, its impact on the food industry will only grow. The integration of robotics in food production and distribution holds the potential to enhance food security, improve quality, and create a more resilient and efficient food system.

13

Chapter 13: The Role of Robotics in Dairy and Livestock Farming

The incorporation of robotics into dairy and livestock farming is transforming the way farmers manage their herds. Robotic milking systems, automated feeding equipment, and health monitoring technologies are enhancing productivity, animal welfare, and farm management practices. These advancements are making dairy and livestock farming more efficient and sustainable.

Robotic milking systems are among the most significant innovations in dairy farming. These systems allow cows to be milked automatically, reducing labor costs and improving milk quality. The robots are equipped with sensors and cameras that ensure a gentle and precise milking process, minimizing stress for the animals. Additionally, the data collected during milking provides valuable insights into each cow's health and milk production.

Automated feeding equipment is also revolutionizing livestock farming. These systems can dispense precise amounts of feed and supplements to each animal based on their nutritional needs. By optimizing feed distribution, farmers can improve animal health, reduce waste, and lower feed costs. Automated feeding systems also free up time for farmers to focus on other important aspects of herd management.

Health monitoring technologies, such as wearable sensors and smart collars, are providing farmers with real-time data on the well-being of their livestock. These devices can track vital signs, activity levels, and behavioral patterns, enabling early detection of illnesses and other health issues. By closely monitoring their animals, farmers can take proactive measures to ensure the health and productivity of their herds.

14

Chapter 14: Innovations in Aquaculture

Aquaculture, or the farming of aquatic organisms, is a rapidly growing sector that is benefiting from technological innovations. Robotics, AI, and biotechnology are being leveraged to enhance the efficiency, sustainability, and scalability of aquaculture operations. These advancements are helping to meet the rising global demand for seafood while minimizing environmental impact.

One of the key innovations in aquaculture is the use of underwater robots for monitoring and maintenance. These robots can navigate fish tanks and ocean pens, capturing high-resolution images and collecting data on water quality, fish health, and infrastructure conditions. The information gathered by underwater robots enables farmers to make informed decisions and address issues promptly, improving overall farm management.

AI-driven analytics are also transforming aquaculture. Machine learning algorithms can analyze data from various sources, such as sensors and cameras, to optimize feeding schedules, monitor growth rates, and detect potential health problems. By leveraging AI, aquaculture operators can enhance productivity, reduce feed waste, and improve the health and welfare of their stock.

Biotechnology is playing a crucial role in developing sustainable aquaculture practices. Genetic engineering and selective breeding techniques are being used to create disease-resistant and fast-growing fish strains. These advancements help to reduce the reliance on antibiotics and minimize the environmental impact of aquaculture. Additionally, innovations in feed formulations, such as plant-based and insect-based feeds, are providing more sustainable alternatives to traditional fishmeal and fish oil.

15

Chapter 15: The Future of Smart Greenhouses

Smart greenhouses are a testament to the potential of technology to revolutionize agriculture. By integrating advanced sensors, automation systems, and data analytics, smart greenhouses provide optimal growing conditions for crops, regardless of external weather conditions. These controlled environments are enabling year-round cultivation, increasing yields, and promoting sustainable farming practices.

Sensors play a critical role in smart greenhouses, continuously monitoring environmental factors such as temperature, humidity, light, and CO_2 levels. These sensors provide real-time data that allows for precise control of the greenhouse environment. Automated systems can adjust lighting, ventilation, and irrigation based on the sensor data, ensuring that crops receive the ideal conditions for growth.

Data analytics and machine learning are enhancing the efficiency of smart greenhouses. By analyzing historical and real-time data, AI algorithms can identify patterns and optimize growing conditions for different crop varieties. This data-driven approach helps to maximize yields, reduce resource consumption, and minimize the environmental impact of greenhouse farming.

Smart greenhouses are also incorporating renewable energy sources, such as solar panels and wind turbines, to reduce their carbon footprint.

Innovations in water recycling and nutrient delivery systems are further promoting sustainability by minimizing water usage and reducing chemical runoff. As technology continues to advance, smart greenhouses hold the potential to play a significant role in addressing global food security and environmental challenges.

Chapter 16: The Role of Robotics in Food Processing

The food processing industry is leveraging robotics to enhance efficiency, consistency, and safety. From automated production lines to quality control systems, robotics is transforming the way food products are prepared, packaged, and delivered. These advancements are streamlining operations, reducing waste, and improving the overall quality of food products.

Automated production lines are at the heart of modern food processing facilities. Robots can perform tasks such as slicing, dicing, mixing, and packaging with high precision and speed. These machines can handle repetitive and labor-intensive processes, reducing the risk of human error and contamination. Automated production lines also enable manufacturers to scale up operations and meet the demands of a growing market.

Robotic quality control systems are ensuring that food products meet high standards of safety and quality. These systems use advanced imaging and sensing technologies to inspect products for defects, contaminants, and inconsistencies. By identifying and removing substandard items, robotic quality control systems help to ensure that consumers receive safe and high-quality food products.

In addition to production and quality control, robotics is playing a role in food packaging and logistics. Automated packaging systems can efficiently wrap, label, and seal products, reducing packaging waste and improving shelf life. Robotics is also being used to optimize warehouse operations and streamline the supply chain, ensuring that food products reach consumers quickly and efficiently.

17

Chapter 17: The Ethical and Social Implications of Food Technology

The rapid advancement of food technology raises important ethical and social questions. As we embrace innovations such as genetic engineering, robotics, and AI, it is essential to consider the potential impact on society, the environment, and future generations. Addressing these ethical and social implications is crucial for ensuring that food technology benefits all stakeholders and promotes a sustainable and equitable food system.

One of the key ethical considerations is the potential impact of food technology on small-scale farmers and rural communities. As large agribusinesses adopt advanced technologies, there is a risk of widening the gap between industrial and small-scale farming. It is important to develop policies and initiatives that support small farmers in accessing and benefiting from new technologies, ensuring that they are not left behind.

The environmental impact of food technology is another critical consideration. While many innovations aim to promote sustainability, there is a need to carefully evaluate their long-term effects on ecosystems and natural resources. Balancing technological advancement with environmental stewardship is essential for achieving sustainable food production.

The use of genetic engineering and biotechnology in food production raises questions about food safety, labeling, and consumer choice. It is important to provide transparent information about genetically modified products and ensure that consumers have the ability to make informed decisions. Additionally, ethical considerations must guide the development and use of these technologies to address potential risks and ensure public trust.

As we navigate the future of food technology, it is essential to engage in inclusive and transparent discussions that consider the perspectives of all stakeholders. By addressing the ethical and social implications of food technology, we can create a food system that is not only innovative and efficient but also equitable and sustainable.

From Farm to Fork to Factory: The Role of Robotics and Society in Food Evolution

Embark on an extraordinary journey through the history of food production, and explore how robotics and society have shaped our relationship with what we eat. **"From Farm to Fork to Factory"** delves into the fascinating evolution of agriculture, from the dawn of farming to the cutting-edge technologies transforming the food industry today.

In this engaging and insightful book, you'll discover how early agricultural practices laid the foundation for modern food production. You'll witness the transformative impact of the Industrial Revolution, the Green Revolution's quest for food security, and the rise of precision agriculture driven by data and technology.

Explore the role of robotics in revolutionizing farming, from autonomous tractors and robotic harvesters to smart greenhouses and vertical farms. Learn how genetic engineering, AI, and food tech startups are pushing the boundaries of what's possible, addressing global challenges such as food security, sustainability, and nutrition.

As you journey through the chapters, you'll encounter thought-provoking discussions on the ethical and social implications of food technology, the intersection of food and society, and the future of sustainable agriculture. Discover how innovations in dairy and livestock farming, aquaculture, and food processing are reshaping the way we produce and consume food.

"From Farm to Fork to Factory" offers a comprehensive and captivating exploration of the past, present, and future of food production. Whether you're a food enthusiast, a tech aficionado, or simply curious about the future of our food systems, this book provides a compelling and informative read that will leave you inspired and enlightened.